An Empower To Strive Series

Contents

Introduction

"Dear Students,

Greetings from the Placement Committee!

The placement fever is all around the campus. The activities for the upcoming placement season (Final year and Summer Internships) have already commenced.
In this context, students should fill their resumes in the format attached to this mail. Students not having work experience may delete the first column, which is Work Experience..."

Every college student in their academic coursework is known to have received this email from their University. Well, we all know how that goes - the University placement committee in its hyper mode of emailing the same resume format to each student, asking them to utilize it to craft an 'original' resume that sets them apart from the crowd.

Oh, the irony!

How about we switch to the other side of this scenario, a few days down the line? Let's take a minute to imagine the plight of the recruiter who sees the exact 'clt+c' and 'clt+v' version of the candidate's summary in their resume.

The question then arises, how can one craft their unique resume to the best of their abilities?

What are those significant points which should be taken care of while drafting a resume?

Can a resume make the difference in getting you your dream job in the first attempt?

Armed with the solutions to such questions and other doubts, let's decode what it takes to craft an effective resume, in your first attempt.

Candidate: "Good morning, can I come in?"

Interviewer: "Good morning, please do, and make yourself comfortable. Can you please pass your documents?"

Candidate: "Absolutely!"

handing over the documents to the interviewer

"This is the application form, and this is my 'resume'."

Interviewer: "I beg your pardon?"

Candidate: *nervously repeating* "Um, this is the application form and the 'resume' as required."

Interviewer: "Oh, alright."

nodding their head in disappointment

And just like that, unbeknownst to the candidate, it was Strike One.

———

During your interview, there is nothing worse than not knowing what you're saying. In this case, the mispronunciation of the word 'resume' in itself may be the only determining factor in the success of your candidature. The term 'resume,' if mispronounced, may prove to act opposite of its meaning!

The correct pronunciation of the word 'resume' is 'rez.juː.meɪ.' (UK) with emphasis on the end 'e' and not 'rɪˈzjuːm' (UK).

The next time you spot someone mispronouncing the word, 'resume' in this context, and make sure that you correct them before they lose their one shot at their dream job.

Now that we've successfully managed to get some potential disasters out of our way, it is now time to address another concern amongst a lot of candidates — the herculean task of figuring out the 'correct' format of a resume. One-click on the wide world of the internet, and one gets bombarded with thousands and thousands of 'correct,' 'right,' 'perfect' (and the adjectives continue) format of the resume.

In case you find yourself stuck in the same web of confusion, let this guidebook be to your rescue. I am not suggesting that this guidebook has THE perfect resume format but rather will act as a step by step guide for you to create a resume that is perfect for your candidature.

Simply put, there exists no perfect resume except for the one which lands you the job.

Let's get it out here, you're creating a resume not to display how awesome you are or justify why you want to switch jobs or to describe how you managed a team of 40. You're creating a resume to land an interview first with the end game of landing the job.

If this doesn't seem obvious, allow me to break it down for you: A graphic designer would have creativity as the central theme for their resume while providing the portfolio link in their resume for allowing the interviewer to have a glance at their work. At the same time, the resume of a business student shall differ by being more practical while focussing on their financial acumen and people skills.

Every job that you wish to apply for demands specific skills which you should possess in your professional profile. A little game of mix and match and highlighting the suitable skills from your profile, you can easily customize your profile according to the job requirements. Resume writing is just perception management at play.

Don't play your candidature; play the job description.

I've elucidated the process of resume writing by breaking it down into five sections, as follows:

1. Resume template. Ahoy! : A one-page template which will prove to be handy for applying to a range of industries right from creatives to coding
2. Breaking down the template: Understanding the five major components of the template, focused on "WHAT" to write as the contents of the resume, one element at a time.
3. Presentation of the Resume: The trick of 4Cs' focused on "HOW" to write the contents of the resume

4. Building up the Resume: An actual resume crafted from utilizing the "WHAT" and "HOW" (followed by ETS 1Up – BONUS tips to put you ahead of the curve)
5. The interviewer's point of view: Analysis of the final resume within six seconds

For ease in comprehension and effective results, we recommend that you pay attention to these five sections in a sequence. However, you may also choose to ignore this series and treat each section in its entirety.

Name Surname

+91-9912345678 | my.email@gmail.com | LinkedIn

SUMMARY Seeking a career in __ sector to gain a comprehensive understanding of the industry as well as the organization while utilizing acquired knowledge and __ skills.

EDUCATION AND SKILLS

Degree (major) | GPA
College/ University, Delhi, India ▪ 2013-2017
Skills:

RELEVANT TRAINING EXPERIENCE

Organization #1 ▪ Delhi, India　　　　**(April 2018 – June 2018)**
(Position Title) Summer Intern
Activity #1
Activity #2

Organization #2 ▪ Mumbai, India　　**(February 2017 – April 2017)**
(Position Title) Intern
Project on "Project Title"
Project Description

ADDITIONAL ACTIVITIES

Sports achievements
Research papers/ Online internships
MOOCs'/ Olympiads
Event organized/ Community Service
Language competency
Soft skills: Leadership/ Team player/ Public speaking

For a downloadable version of the template, log on to Empower to Strive: (https://www.empowertostrive.com/)

With the current focus on the "WHAT" to include in a resume, let's understand the five essential components of the Resume template.

Introduction

Name Surname
+91-9912345678 | my.email@gmail.com | LinkedIn

This topmost part of the resume should include your contact information inclusive of your name, phone number, and email. As suggestive from the picture, your name holds the most significant text size in the resume, which allows attracting direct attention to it. The text size of 18 for the title (name) with the body size of 12 should ideally work.

You should follow up with your phone number, which should be functional and not suffer from network outages.

Next is your email ID, which precedes your LinkedIn ID. It is wise to have a professional email ID mentioned in your resume, one that your college has provided you. What this also suggests is that in case you are still using the first-ever emails of your life, which you created for yourselves – the days of being 'Cool.Rahul@gmail.com' or 'AkshayRocks@hotmail.com' or 'CutePriya@xyz.com,' they all need to be let go. It would also be wise not to have your birthday information in your email. The aim is to portray yourself to be as professional as possible.

> **ETS 1Up:** In today's digital world, the chances of your resume shared virtually is more in comparison to the paperback formats. With that in mind, mentioning your LinkedIn ID while hyperlinking your profile on your resume would allow any recruiter to get to know more about you and not get confined in that one sheet of paper.

How could you leverage LinkedIn to serve to the best of your abilities? Well, that is a different topic altogether.

Summary

SUMMARY Seeking a career in __ sector to gain a comprehensive understanding of the industry as well as the organization while utilizing acquired knowledge and __ skills.

This next part offers you a chance to convince the interviewer about your candidature being the right fit for the job. For this, make sure that your summary is custom made for the role you are planning to apply. The summary also happens to be the first proper sentence that the interviewer shall read off your resume. You must make the sentence error-free and purpose packed. Consider this part of the resume as your elevator pitch on paper.

By answering the following questions, you can get ideas for your written elevator pitch.

- "What makes you a suitable candidate for this position?"
- "How do your qualifications aid the potential employer?"

Another concern which many candidates face is the choice to include a summary in their resume or not. Well, its inclusion is not necessary and purely depends on you. In case you are sure that your summary is hitting the bull's eye with the target job profile, then it is a good idea to add it. However, on the other hand, writing a summary takes up space too, which you should wisely compromise on.

EDUCATION AND SKILLS
Degree (major) | GPA College/ University, Delhi, India ▪ 2013-2017 Skills:

The third part of the resume mentions your educational qualifications and academic skills.

For the sake of being relevant, you should follow reverse chronology while mentioning your achievements in the resume. In the case of academic degrees, the latest degree awarded to you should be mentioned first and then the degree previous to this one and so on. For example, a PhD. should be written first followed by masters and then a bachelor and then high school and so on.

In this section, you should begin by writing about the last degree which you completed or the degree which you are currently pursuing. In the (majors) section next to the degree, mention the specialization you have pursued or are pursuing, e.g., marketing, operations, sales, food engineering, mechanical engineering, computer science, etc.

Next is your GPA or your CGPA score. It is wise not to mention a score lower than 7, for you don't know the nature of the interviewer scoring your profile. In most cases, low scores are looked down upon, so it would make sense for you to avoid altogether mentioning them, however, at the same time presenting your academic skills and other projects in such a manner that they compensate for the low scores. In the case that your college/ university follows the percentage scoring, you can mention your grades in % then.

Next is the name of the college or University from where you pursued or are pursuing an academic degree. The duration of the course follows this in terms of start and end year. You can mention the end year in case you have already completed the degree, or in case you are still pursuing the course, you can specify "Present" in the end year of the course.

For the skills section, the idea is to mention the top 3-4 hard skills which you are confident you would be able to defend via your work. Make sure these skills are relevant to both the role that you're applying for and the degree that you're pursuing.

RELEVANT TRAINING EXPERIENCE	
Organization #1 ▪ Delhi, India	**(April 2018 – June 2018)**
(Position Title) Summer Intern	
Activity #1	
Activity #2	
Organization #2 ▪ Mumbai, India	**(February 2017 – April 2017)**
(Position Title) Intern	
Project on "Project Title"	
Project Description	

In this section, you can mention about the internships and projects that you did during your college coursework. One way of doing this - begin with the organization and the city where you interned, followed by your title during that internship. You should highlight 1 or 2 significant tasks that you did during your time there.

The trick in writing this section is not just to show that you were an intern at the organization but how resourceful you were during that period.

The duration of the internship can be mentioned through the beginning and the end month and not through the specific dates. By choosing this, you can skip mentioning the number of months you did the internship.

Sometimes, candidates choose to undertake a research project and not an institutional internship. In that case, it would be appropriate to mention the goals and skills developed while pursuing the research.

If you have 2-3 internships under your belt, you can mention those in a reverse chronology order.

The key to making this section successful is mentioning only those projects which are relevant to the role that you are actively applying. For example, in case you interned as a content writer at some organization, then it would make sense to mention this internship when you are applying for the position of a social media marketer and not a Quality Research Analyst.

Extracurricular/ Additional Activities

ADDITIONAL ACTIVITIES
Sports achievements
Research papers/ Online internships
MOOCs'/ Olympiads
Event organized/ Community Service
Language competency
Soft skills: Leadership/ Team player/ Public speaking

The resume should ideally have the extracurricular activities towards the end. One reason why this section is crucial and should be paid substantial attention to is that it brings the 'human' to a piece of paper.

Think for a second here; the candidate has hundreds of applications for a particular position, what should they use as a distinguishing factor to set the candidature apart?

The extracurricular section is when you get to set yourself apart from the crowd just based on your personality. In this section, you should talk about the co-curricular activities that you participated in, on-off college, your hobbies, your interests, your quirks while making sure that they fit the bill of being professional.

For the case of a typical Indian cricket fan interested in mentioning this in their resume, 'watching cricket' would come off as immature and unprofessional. By expressing the same sentiment as "cricket enthusiast," you would allow the interviewer to ask your questions about this interest – "I see you are a cricket enthusiast, do you play cricket?" The candidate can then use this opportunity to further talk about this in detail and maybe impress the interviewer by quoting facts about the interview's favorite cricketer. Such tweaking gives the candidate a chance to strike up a conversation during an interview by giving them a chance to impress the interviewer via their personality.

For indicating your knowledge about coding languages, you should mention proficiency levels too. For example, write Java (Proficient), C++ (Beginner), and C (Beginner) instead of Java, C++, and C.

Stick to mentioning the top 2-3 skills of yours which you think to define your persona best. You should also use this section to specify your soft skills – Teamwork, leadership, public speaking, negotiations, which will add to your candidature.

By the end of this section, you would have given the interviewer enough armor to judge not only your educational capabilities but also take a genuine interest in your personality.

Presentation of the Resume

With understanding the "WHAT" part of the resume, it is time to make the resume look presentable i.e., the "HOW" part. One way of doing this is by understanding the concept of 4Cs'.

1. Clean
2. Clear
3. Crisp
4. Concise

1. Clean is the way you should present your resume for it to flow and be easy on the eyes of the interviewer. To ensure this, the font size and font type should be readable and aesthetically pleasing. Stick to using fonts such as Arial, Times New Roman, Georgia, or Calibri. It is not a good idea to use more than two different fonts in your resume. A font size of 12 should be the right choice for the body of your resume (Never go lower than point 11 font) with your name in the resume written in font size 16. By making the name the largest font in the resume, you are making sure that your identity remains the topmost priority in the resume. Put extra effort into maintaining margins around the resume to allow adequate white space in the resume. Use a margin of 0.5 inches for displaying the top part of your resume and then work your way down. This way, you will be able to avoid getting missed by the

Applicant Tracking Software (ATS) employed by the interviewer.

2. Clear is the quality of information you are presenting to the interviewer. Most importantly, the information you provide must be accurate. Make sure the hierarchy is established, i.e., you write the data in reverse chronological order. For instance, the coursework you pursued or the grade you studied last should be mentioned first. In the case of your grade 10th and 12th, you should write class 12th first, followed by grade 10th next. This is the reverse chronology.

3. Crisp is being to the point and avoids long sentences. You can utilize bullet points to present the information in a structured manner. However, make sure to not use more than three bullet points per section as that would negate their innate purpose. Using bold or italics on the text can help to highlight the required quality in your candidature, efficiently.

4. Concise is about maintaining brevity. One good rule is keeping your resume within 1 page to accommodate the short second attention span of the interviewer. The information you provide in the resume should be well articulated and self-explanatory. One way to do this is by avoiding jargon. Jargons are technical terms specific to your

field/ industry. If everything fails, remember the phrase 'KISS' – Keep It Simple, Silly.

Now, how about we bring everything together and create an actual resume?

Aparna Sharma

+91-9912345678 | aparna.sharma@gmail.com | LinkedIn

SUMMARY Seeking a career in the Retail sector to gain a comprehensive understanding of the industry and the organization while utilizing acquired knowledge and strong interpersonal skills.

EDUCATION AND SKILLS

(BBA) Bachelor of Business Administration | Marketing | GPA: 7/10
WOW College, Delhi, India ▪ 2017 - Present
Skills: Sales & Integrated Marketing, Customer service, Merchandising

RELEVANT TRAINING EXPERIENCE

Prominent Mall ▪ Delhi, India
(April 2018 – June 2018)
Summer Intern at the Marketing Department
1. Created a 'Mall Marketing Framework' for tracking the marketing activities, i.e., event execution, campaign engagement, social media analysis, footfall promotion strategy for 0.6 million sq. Ft. Mall
2. Implemented NPS (Net Promoter Score) template to track the retention rate and profitability of mall patrons.

BestWear ▪ Mumbai, India
(February 2017 – April 2017)
Short term Project at Sales Department
Part of a five-member team to carry out a project on "Correlation between sales and customer service" for the Brand BestWear

---

ADDITIONAL ACTIVITIES

1. MOOCs': Brand Management, 2016 (Coursera); Poetry, 2017 (EdX)
2. Organized 'Manthan' Event for 100 Kathak enthusiasts after securing a sponsorship worth Rs. 2,00,000/- during Youth Festival, December 2017
3. Language competency: English, Hindi, and Punjabi
4. Volunteer for NGO, Ek Parivaar (One Family) during the weekends

A commonly asked question is whether one should have a picture of themselves on the resume. It is recommended to absolutely avoid adding your image to your resume, especially in the Indian job scenario. However, if you wish to add one, make sure the picture is formatted well, professionally taken, and looks like you-have-got-what- it-takes-to- be-hired pose.

Quantify the facts: Remove all the extra adjectives you use to toot your own horn in the resume and instead opt for stating facts about your accomplishments. To explain better via an example, "Organized 'Manthan' Event for 100 Kathak enthusiasts after securing a sponsorship worth Rs. 2,00,000/- during Youth Festival, December 2017" is an effective way of presenting your skills than just showing the same fact as, "I displayed leadership qualities when I organized a dance event, Manthan in 2017". The former way of presentation is a more memorable, quantifiable and reliable way for the interviewer to assess your skills.

Another interesting example would be, "Co-developed material for heat radiators that saved ₹ 300,000 per year" instead of "Part of the R&D Team" or "Conducted process mapping studies to improve throughput by 36 percent and ensure compliance with customer specifications" instead of "Ensured compliance to improve customer satisfaction". This is the real power of numbers!

Enlisted below are some action verbs you should use to derive more impact from your quantifying activity on your job actions.

Achieved	Delivered	Grew
Added	Eliminated	Improved
Awarded	Exceeded	Increased
Changed	Expanded	Introduced
Contributed	Gained	Maximized
Decreased	Generated	Minimized

You can also use the following type of verbs to bring about the same effect off your job responsibilities.

Increased x by %	Decreased x by %	Improved x by $
Reduced x by $	Introduced new x that led to # more	Successfully added # new x

In case you're applying for a position involving the creative media and coding field, you should add links to your online portfolios or blogs. However, no one would want to open a link and see the latest update, one-year-old. That is why you need to be responsible for keeping your portfolios up to date and thorough and, at the same time, make sure that the web link works.

You really need to work on conducting enough Spellchecks and proof reading the content at least thrice. One small mistake and it will speak about your attention to detail. For this, you can use tools like Grammarly.

For the achievements/ accomplishments section, do not mention your school achievements just for the sake of filling up that column. Activities such as winning the painting competition in grade 6th or maybe attending a summer camp in grade 10th come off as immature and unprofessional. You can, however, mention your divisional rank in Olympiads, state-level participation in sports, representation in extracurricular activities that dignifies your thought process, and adds credibility to your candidature.

At the same time, what is professional is creating an engaging LinkedIn account and hyperlinking it right in your resume! By adopting such a trick, you invite the interviewer to know more about you (in case they want) by clicking on that link, and well, it sets you precedent of how serious you are about your career.

Trust me; this one will take your resume miles ahead.

That is it! When you think you've created your resume, hand it to your friend to read it. If the impression off your resume in their first 20 seconds of reading it, reflects your goals and qualifications, then congratulations, job well done!!

They say, less is better and how! Recent findings show that it takes an interviewer, just 6 seconds to scan through a resume and take the decision to read it in detail or not! Imagine, a mere 6 seconds, and only a piece of paper decides your fate!

A pro-tip to take full advantage of this finding is to limit your resume within one page unless your work experience is more than ten years. However, in the case, your work experience is less than ten years, cramming up your quality content within one page will not take you far. It would be a better decision to distribute your resume into two pages evenly. In case your resume is more than one page, it would be wise to repeat your contact information on all pages. This way, in case the interviewer wants to get in touch with you later, they could avoid the scrambling involved in getting your contact information.

We have taken the liberty of collating some thoughts from industry recruiters to understand what they like to see when they evaluate resumes.

- "Simple and consistent formatting."
- "I like to see solid examples of work done and tasks accomplished."
- "Statements that quantify the work that they have done."
- Involvement in activities outside of coursework – volunteering, groups, sports, etc."

- "Listing of relevant experience and organizations which fit the role they're applying for."
- "Duration of work experience at each job indicating whether they are a job hopper or steady goer."
- "Adding well maintained and engaging LinkedIn profile to the job application is cheery on the cake."
- "Well articulated description of the work listed in the resume."

For the final chapter, let's get into the shoes of the interviewing experts and experiment with analyzing a full-fledged resume within 6 seconds to empathize with them and see what they mean!

With an actual resume in place, let's try to analyze some workings in the resume.

holds the resume in hand

Second 1

Aparna Sharma – Strong interpersonal skills – Consistent formatting – Ample white spaces

Second 2

BBA in Marketing – 7 GPA – Skills are a match – No Master's degree

Second 3 & Second 4

Two relevant internships of 3 months duration each – Skills in the first internship (Marketing, NPS) implemented for a sizeable area (0.6 mil sq. ft. area) – worked with a reputed brand for 2nd internship – project conducted in line with job description offered

Second 5

Pursues MOOCs' – demonstrates strong leadership skills by securing sponsorship for organizing an event – Multilingual – volunteering work aligns with organization values

Second 6

No typos – well-articulated resume – candidate seems like a good fit - Selected

keeps the resume down

Needless to say, the candidate indeed was a piece of paper...

Applicant Tracking Software and your fate

With the advent of computers and automation, the recruiting agencies have one-upped themselves, too, and how! Gone are the days of recruiters reading resumes line by line to shortlist the proposals.

You know you are dealing with an applicant tracking software when you fill in details of your candidate even after you've submitted your resume. Welcome to the future (rather the modern reality) of the resume selection process.

What is ATS, and how do they work?

ATS, or also known as Talent Management Systems, are relatively common these days to automate the hiring process and process job applications, faster. Amongst the hundreds, if not thousands of job applicants received by a recruiting manager, ATS proves to be a faster and more scientific way of screening candidates.

With ATS in place, gone are the days of organizations wasting their time and effort for sorting and filing the paperwork.

For the recruiters, ATS allows them to review applications, send out prompts for online evaluations, and push out notifications indicating the status of their fate – either a rejection or a job offer!

Most ATS software allows input of information right from a professional networking site, which proves to be a time saving for the candidates. The candidate can then add more impact to their application by customizing it further rather than filling the necessary information over and over.

While this process tilts more in favor of the recruiters than the candidates, one needs to beat the increased adoption of this automated process at its own game.

Majority of the Fortune 500 companies utilize the wonders of ATS systems. In fact, Workday, Taleo, Success Factors are some of the most commonly used ATS system used by Fortune 500 companies.

1. Ranking and Relevance: Each job opportunity comes with a job description that should be analyzed well, and then the resume is applied. After you upload your resume and input relevant details on the website, the ATS kicks into the picture and starts scanning the information for a better match.

   Taleo, one of the ATS systems, uses a feature, "Req Rank," which indicates the percentage of the relevance of the resume with the job description. This way, the recruiter can focus on the top 5-6 candidates to evaluate instead of reading all the applications, thus managing their time effectively.

2. Keywording your resume: One other way of filtering the applications is by searching for a specific title or skill relevant to the job profile. For example, let's say for the role of a store manager, "SAAS" and "sales" is the applied filter, and your resume doesn't have either of them, tough luck!

   A search can contain multiple terms such as those mentioned above, either individually or in combination.

   Hence, it is crucial to customize your resume to the job you're applying for while predicting the right keywords relevant to the job.

3. Use both long forms and acronyms of standard terms such as **"Search Engine Optimization** *(SEO),"* for you never know which keyword will be used as a filter by the recruiter.

4. Use standard fonts **Arial**, Times New Roman, **Georgia**, and limit them to 2 fonts per resume to avoid parsing errors.

5. Avoid making your resume fancy and stick to standard headings. Focus on getting past the ATS systems first and then can you try your hand at impressing the interviewer with your persona.

When you upload your resume onto a website, it isn't always necessary that the recruiter will read your resume, line by line and, as is. With ATS systems in picture, the resume is 'read' as a digital profile as it has been trained to read. What that essentially means is the chances that the recruiter misses reading almost entire parts of the resume becomes high!

You have to create an ATS friendly resume by keeping the format of the resume, wait for it – Clean, Clear, Crisp and Concise.

Keep the formatting of the resume consistent, format standard, and document type, exact. More importantly, avoid overstuffing your resume with keywords to beat the ATS systems.

Chances are you'd be caught by the recruiter even though you'd pass the ATS test. Focus on creating a resume matching your actual experiences, intelligently.

The ATS isn't going anywhere anytime soon. It is just getting better and better with the advancements in Artificial Intelligence. It would be best if you kept up the way ATS works for clearing this war would be the definite first step, which will get you to sit in front of the recruiter for an interview opportunity.

Who is this book for?

It takes an interviewer just under 6 seconds to scan a resume and decide if they want to read it thoroughly or not!

With such a paucity of time, it sure becomes a herculean task for a candidate to present the 'right' things the 'right way' to the interviewer.

Akin to the trailer of a movie, this book empowers the reader with all the right elements along with the methods of presenting them, required for crafting an ideal resume, which will give the interviewer a glimpse of the candidate's professional story.

In today's cut-throat competitive world where millions of job seekers eye the same prize, this book will serve to be of use to the candidates wanting to win the job by standing out in the crowd. Best suited for college grads taking on their first jobs, employees looking to make a career switch and job placement institutions and corporate relation committees of universities and colleges, this book is a must-have.

Best aided with active networking to back up your candidature for a role, this book shows you how to stand out in the crowd by showcasing a laser approach on your unique skills and individual accomplishments and eventually winning your dream job!

About Empower To Strive

Empower to Strive (The Growth Mindset Blog) was born from the need to help humans become a better version of themselves.

We are a positive online community which works together to point out our shortcomings yet celebrates our collective will to get better at who we are, every single day.

BECAUSE [1.01^365 > 0.99^365]

If you are ready to strive towards a better life and in the process, empower others to do the same, welcome to the club!

Let us together, **Empower to Strive** :)

Head on to https://www.empowertostrive.com/ for more resources and valuable content!

www.ingramcontent.com/pod-product-compliance
Lightning Source LLC
Chambersburg PA
CBHW031505210526
45463CB00003B/1091